DATE DUE

DODD, MEAD WONDERS BOOKS

Wonders of the Weather by Tex Antoine
Wonders of the Mosquito World by Phil Ault
Wonders of Animal Migration by Jacquelyn Berrill
Wonders of Animal Nurseries by Jacquelyn Berrill
Wonders of the Antarctic by Jacquelyn Berrill
Wonders of the Monkey World by Jacquelyn Berrill
Wonders of the Arctic by Jacquelyn Berrill
Wonders of the Fields and Ponds at Night by Jacquelyn Berrill
Wonders of the Seashore by Jacquelyn Berrill
Wonders of the Woods and Desert at Night by Jacquelyn Berrill
Wonders of the World of Wolves by Jacquelyn Berrill
Wonders Inside You by Margaret Cosgrove
Wonders of the Tree World by Margaret Cosgrove
Wonders Under a Miscroscope by Margaret Cosgrove
Wonders of Your Senses by Margaret Cosgrove
Wonders of the Reptile World by Helen Gere Cruickshank
Wonders of the Rivers by Virginia S. Eifert
Wonders Beyond the Solar System by Rocco Feravolo
Wonders of Gravity by Rocco Feravolo
Wonders of Mathematics by Rocco Feravolo
Wonders of Sound by Rocco Feravolo
Wonders of the Heavens by Kenneth Heuer
Wonders of the World of Shells by Morris K. Jacobson and William K. Emerson
Wonders of Heat and Light by Owen S. Lieberg
Wonders of Magnets and Magnetism by Owen S. Lieberg
Wonders of Animal Architecture by Sigmund A. Lavine
Wonders of Animal Disguises by Sigmund A. Lavine
Wonders of the Anthill by Sigmund A. Lavine
Wonders of the Bat World by Sigmund A. Lavine
Wonders of the Beetle World by Sigmund A. Lavine
Wonders of the Fly World by Sigmund A. Lavine
Wonders of the Hive by Sigmund A. Lavine
Wonders of the Owl World by Sigmund A. Lavine
Wonders of the Spider World by Sigmund A. Lavine
Wonders of the Wasp's Nest by Sigmund A. Lavine
Wonders of the Dinosaur World by William H. Matthews III
Wonders of Fossils by William H. Matthews III
Wonders of Sand by Christie McFall
Wonders of Snow and Ice by Christie McFall
Wonders of Stones by Christie McFall
Wonders of Gems by Richard M. Pearl
Wonders of Rocks and Minerals by Richard M. Pearl
Wonders of the Butterfly World by Hilda Simon
Wonders of Hummingbirds by Hilda Simon
Wonders of Our National Parks by Peter Thomson
Wonders of Flight by Robert Wells

ILLUSTRATED WITH PHOTOGRAPHS AND DRAWINGS

Wonders of
the World of Shells

SEA, LAND, AND FRESH-WATER

Morris K. Jacobson and William K. Emerson

DODD, MEAD & COMPANY • NEW YORK

PICTURE CREDITS

American Museum of Natural History, frontispiece, 14, 15, 16, 23, 25, 31, 36, 37, 39, 43, 45, 46, 47, 50, 57, 61, 64; Arthur H. Clarke, National Museum of Canada, 18; John E. Jacobson, 8, 69; Morris K. Jacobson, 10, 67; S. Kawaguti and T. Yamasu, 48; D. Laursen, 21; Warren J. Osterwald, 71; George Raeihle, Elmhurst, New York, 13, 24, 28, 33; Rudolf Stohler, Berkeley, California, 27; R. Turner and J. Rosewater, 55.

TO KENNY AND ELANA

who even when little loved sea shells

Contents

Author Jacobson showing his grandchildren, Elana and Kenny, how to look for shells on the beach.

I

Introduction to
the Wonders of Mollusks

When you go to the seashore for a vacation or even a shorter visit, among the first things you can expect to find on the beach are sea shells. Some are curved like dishes or boats, others are round or shaped like little spinning tops, and still others are long and slender, like fat needles. There are also many more kinds of shells of innumerable shapes and sizes, some so small and delicate that they have to be looked for very carefully. Frequently, they are very beautifully colored. This is a common experience. Everybody knows that sea shells are found on the seashore. But some people are pleasantly surprised when they also see shells on the shores of lakes and ponds or near the banks of streams and rivers. And they are even more surprised when they discover that some shells are found on trees, in fields, in forests, in the deserts, and on mountaintops.

Of course, it is wrong to call the terrestrial and fresh-water species "sea shells," since they do not live in or near the sea. All these shells, whether found in the sea, in fresh water or on land, are the shells of a large and enormously interesting group of a division of the Animal Kingdom called Mollusca, the mollusks. The name comes from the Latin word *mollis* which means soft, because although the shell is hard, the animal which builds it is mushy and soft-bodied. Anybody who has ever eaten a clam or oyster on the half shell—both these delicious animals are mollusks—will know exactly what we mean.

Field trip of the New York Shell Club to a Staten Island beach which has been exposed by low tide.

When we say the mollusk builds the shell, we do not mean it builds in the way that we humans or beavers or birds or even bees build places in which to live. The limy shell material is secreted; that is, formed by special glands in each mollusk. As the lime comes in contact with the air or water, it hardens into the shell, very much like concrete in a wooden form, only much faster. But the mollusk needs no wooden form for its shell design. It builds it as unconsciously as we build our own bony skeletons.

Since mollusks are living animals, they act like all living animals. They have to be born, to feed, to protect themselves, to grow, to reproduce themselves, to get older, and, finally, to die. They do some of these things in ways which may seem peculiar to us. In this book, we will describe the strange life habits of many kinds of mollusks.

There are people who always like to know the role certain animals play in our world of nature. They mean, of course, of what use or good are they to us humans? Economists and scientists also ask this question, but instead of asking of what use animals are, they talk about their "economic importance." This means in what way are they harmful. These are fair questions and we will try to answer them in this book.

But there is still another way of looking at nonhuman life. We need not always think about the usefulness or even beauty and interest of animals to us. The other animals, big and small, are here on earth—they inhabit the world together with us. They are our fellow creatures that also contribute to the balance of nature. They live for themselves, in ways that are different, yet basically very much like our own. Therefore, even though we will say something about useful and harmful mollusks, we will say much more about mollusks as creatures of the Animal Kingdom, with which intelligent persons should be familiar.

After reading this introduction to the wonders of the world of molluscan life, we hope that you will desire to learn more about these fascinating creatures. Perhaps you will start gathering shells and join the legion of completely and pleasantly "shell shocked" collectors.

2

The Classes of Mollusks

Long before the first animals with bony internal skeletons appeared in the seas, there were some creatures who were building tiny shelters to protect their soft bodies. For this purpose they made use of the calcium and other minerals dissolved in the waters around them. The soft-bodied coral polyps combined their individually small shelters to form reefs and islands. But many other animals built separate covers in which they lived and which they carried around with them like suits of armor. These shelters are called external skeletons or exoskeletons, to distinguish them from the internal or endoskeletons found in fish, amphibians, reptiles, birds, and mammals. The latter animals are known as the vertebrates. Invertebrates are animals without internal backbones or skeletons. They have external ones instead.

Since exoskeletons are the actual skeletons of invertebrates, they are generally closely attached to the animal's body. If the exoskeleton is forcibly removed, the soft-bodied animal cannot live.

There are many different types of animals that have exoskeletons. Approximately ninety-five per cent of the species living at the present time are invertebrates. Included in these are the crustaceans, such as crabs, lobsters, shrimps, and barnacles; many insects, like beetles; and protozoans, such as forams, which are hardly larger than the head of a pin. Among the animals that have made the most successful use of such exoskeletons are the mollusks, the best known of which are the clams, oysters, scallops, mussels, and snails.

Zoologists divide all the shelled mollusks into six different classes.

A live moon snail (gastropod); note the large fleshy foot and the tentacles and mantle extended.

These can be easily recognized by the type of shell or exoskeleton which each builds—or does not build—as we shall see. Here is a brief description of each of these six classes.

It is pretty well known that all clams have two shells which open on hinges like doors. So these mollusks are put into a class called bivalves, a word which means two valves or shells.

Snails have only one shell and, for a long time, they were called univalves or one-shelled. Soon it was seen, however, that several very different kinds of mollusks also have only one shell, so the general term univalve was discarded. Instead, each one-shelled group has its own distinguishing or descriptive name.

Snails move along on the lower part of their bodies. They appear to travel on their stomachs. Since the animal seems to use its stomach for its foot, a scientist made up the name gastropod for the second class of mollusks. This word is a combination of the

13

Greek words *gastro,* stomach, and *poda,* foot (like in the name podiatrist for a foot doctor). Anyone who watches a snail or slug move along, will see how fitting the term gastropod is for these creatures. Most gastropod shells, whether high or low, are twisted into graceful spirals, like a winding staircase. But limpet shells are low and not twisted. They look like inverted cups or Chinese hats.

The members of the third class of mollusks also have a single shell, but this shell looks very much like a small elephant tusk. It reminded some scientists of a boat, so the word scaphopod or boat-footed was invented for them, from the Greek work *skaphos,* meaning boat, joined with *poda* or foot. *Skaphos* is also part of another Greek word meaning digger. Since all scaphopods dig in sand or mud, this is a very good name for them.

The fourth class of mollusks also has a single shell. This shell is not all in one piece. It is formed of eight overlapping and interlocking shelly plates which are held together by a strong surrounding band or girdle. The shelled mollusks in this class are called chitons. *Chiton* was the Greek name for the outer shirtlike garment worn by the men in classical times. Perhaps this word was selected by the scientists because the shell of a chiton can be bent like a piece of clothing. It is not stiff and immovable as the shell of an ordinary snail is. A chiton can roll itself up like an armadillo when it is taken from the rock on which it rests. The chitons form the major group of the larger class Polyplacophora, a name derived

An elephant tusk shell (scaphopod).

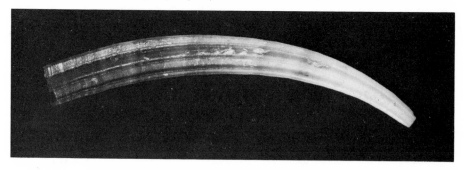

A chiton or pill-bug mollusk.

from the Greek words *poly,* meaning many, and *placophora,* for plate bearer.

Octopuses, cuttlefish, and squid seem to have their tentacles growing right out of their heads. Since the tentacles can be looked upon as a kind of foot, these animals are put into the fifth class called cephalopods. The first part of the name comes from the Greek word *kephalos,* which means head. The second part is that now familiar foot, hence these are head-footed animals. The exoskeleton has been lost in the course of evolution by most living species of cephalopods. In ancient times, many millions of years ago, most cephalopods did have large, flatly coiled, beautiful shells, some of which are still being found as fossils in many parts of the world. Today, only the pearly nautilus still has an external skeleton. The paper nautilus may also carry a shell but it is not used, as is the case with most mollusks, to protect the soft body. It has a different

15

An argonaut (cephalopod) with egg case (model).

purpose. When the eggs are laid, they are placed in this lovely shell-like receptacle and carried by the mother until they hatch. The shell is only an egg case. The animal is not connected to the shell, but it holds it in place by two large tentacles which also deposit the paperlike material out of which the shell is formed.

As we have said, none of the other living cephalopods have external skeletons. Cephalopods are able to move through the water as a jet plane flies through the air. Squids are sometimes called sea arrows for this reason. A heavy exoskeleton would be a big hindrance to such movement. Therefore the cephalopods have lost an external shell and, instead, have a small internal one. Among these internally shelled cephalopods is the cuttlefish, the bones of which are hung in canary cages to supply the birds with the calcium which they need in their diet.

So far, we have mentioned the bivalves (Bivalvia), the gastro-

16

pods (Gastropoda), the scaphopods (Scaphopoda), the chitons (Polyplacophora), and the cephalopods (Cephalopoda). These five are the most important groups of shelled mollusks. The sixth class is very small. It was thought to have died out eons ago. But recently some examples of these rare mollusks were found alive. These primitive animals live in very deep water off the coasts of the New World and elsewhere. They are called Monoplacophora. The word, a combination of three Greek words, means single (*mono*) plate (*placo*) carriers (*phora*). It fits these mollusks because they have only a single shell and look quite like an ordinary limpet. Why are they put into a separate class? The reason is a little complicated—but interesting.

Some zoologists believe that the mollusks are related to certain kinds of worms. Both the worms and the mollusks have a common ancestor. These worms are called annelids and include the earthworm, whose body is composed of many sections or segments. Of all the different kinds of mollusks, only the Monoplacophora have signs of such segmented bodies. Instead of having a single pair of gills and kidneys, they have five or six pairs, on opposite sides of their bodies. In a way then the Monoplacophora can be regarded

A squid (cephalopod) catching a fish (model).

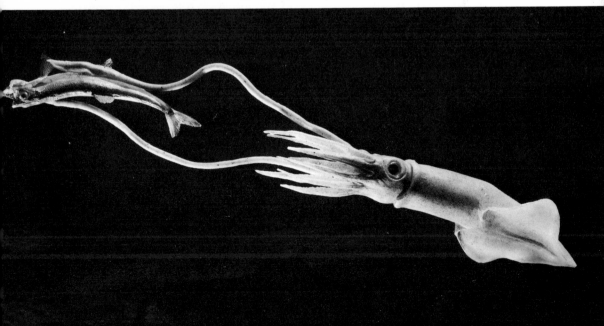

The segmented mollusk (Monoplacophora).

as the "missing link" between the annelid worms and the mollusks. They have a shell like a mollusk but a segmented body like a worm, hence the popular name, gastroverm, probably shortened from gastropod-verm or snail-worm, was recently proposed for them.

So we see that there are six classes of mollusks in which all or part of the living members have an external skeleton, that is a shell: bivalves (the clams, the mussels and their relatives), gastropods (the limpets, snails, and slugs), scaphopods (the elephant-tusk shells), chitons (the roll-up snails), cephalopods (the octopuses, cuttlefish, and squids), and the segmented mollusks (Mono-placophora, or gastroverms).

3

The Life of Mollusks

WHERE THEY LIVE

The mollusks appeared very early in geological history. Many groups of them have died out, as have the dinosaurs and trilobites. But many other groups have taken their places, so mollusks have steadily increased in variety and numbers. Only insects exceed them in the number of species living at the present time. There are thought to be more kinds of mollusks alive today than at any other single period in the geological record.

Mollusks live everywhere—in the seas, the rivers, ponds and lakes, and even on land. The only element they have not colonized is the air. There are no flying mollusks. Most of them live only in the sea, where members of all six classes can be found. In fresh water, we find only two of the six classes, bivalves and gastropods. There are no fresh-water chitons, scaphopods, cephalopods or monoplacophorans. And on the land, the only mollusks to be seen are the gastropods.

Some mollusks swim, some crawl, and some jet propel themselves through the water. Some can burrow in sand, rocks, and wood. Some construct nests of sand grains and weeds. Mollusks live in the deepest seas and have been discovered as high as 15,000 feet in the mountains. On land, they occur practically everywhere, in small numbers. They live in lush tropical rain forests, in barren deserts, and even in city lots and parks. Some live in the Arctic, while others flourish in the hot water of boiling springs. A few also occur deep in caves where, because of the absence of light, they are blind, like some species of cave dwelling fish.

A story is told about a famous malacologist, that is, a zoologist who specializes in the study of mollusks, who was once crossing the country in a train. In a barren part of western Kansas, the train suddenly came to a stop because of some mechanical trouble. The malacologist did not feel like spending all his time waiting in the train, so he climbed down and began to examine the ground under his feet. To his delight, among the broken stones which formed the roadbed, he found and began to collect hundreds of small to tiny mollusks. This malacologist was one passenger who did not mind the time lost because the train had been delayed.

Most marine mollusks live on coral and rocks or in the sand or mud near the shore. Some species, however, thrive only at the bottom of the ocean, many thousands of feet deep. That is where, as we remember, Monoplacophora lives. There are also certain "floating" mollusks which live only in the open sea and never reach the bottom or the shore. As a matter of fact, if they are forced on land by storms or tides they die.

How are such mollusks able to keep afloat? Many weigh very little and have very thin, glassy shells, which enables them to float with ease. Others can swim about rather vigorously almost like a fish.

But there is one kind of snail that cannot float or swim easily and yet it, too, manages to live on the surface of the sea. The beautiful purple or violet snail called *Janthina*, looks like a typical gastropod, but it spends its entire life floating on the sea surface, like a piece of driftwood or bladder seaweed. It manages to do this simply by building a little raft for itself and keeps afloat by holding on to this. The raft is made of a kind of slime which *Janthina* gives off. As the slime oozes out, the snail forms it into little bubbles which rapidly harden in the air. Many such bubbles are made until they form a real raft. *Janthina* does not ride on the raft like Huckleberry Finn. It holds on with a part of its foot and floats upside down alongside.

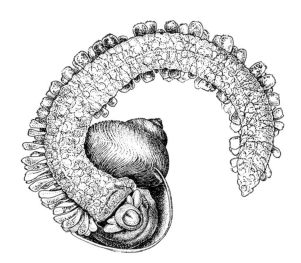

A *violet snail* (Janthina) *with its floating raft; seen from above.*

Janthina also uses the raft for another purpose. Its eggs are laid in capsules and these capsules are then attached to the bottom of the raft. Thus the raft keeps the snail from sinking and protects the eggs until they hatch.

Each *Janthina* does not float along all alone. Huge numbers of snails join their rafts together until many hundreds of square feet of the sea are covered by a floating armada of *Janthina*. In this way, the violet snail can spend its entire life in safety—unless a storm comes along and blows the raft on shore. When that happens, a whole beach is covered with thousands of beautifully colored snails which quickly die. Once ashore, there is no hope for them. They cannot crawl back into the sea. Shell collectors in Florida have written about such events—lucky for them, not so lucky for the snails! These events the collectors call "The Wreck of the Good Ship *Janthina*."

All shell-bearing mollusks, as we know, need lime to build their exoskeletons or shells. This lime is found in the food they eat, in the soil in which they live, or in the waters which surround them. Where the land is poor in lime, as in granitic soils, snails are scarce or, if they do live there, have very thin and fragile shells. In such areas, snails get their lime by scraping it from the shells of dead mollusks or sometimes even from their living brothers.

One tiny gastropod, which looks like a wheat grain, has found a way of getting its lime, a way which we might consider to be rather gruesome. It is usually found burrowing in the soil—and the ground it prefers is near cemeteries! Here this diminutive mollusk is able to make use of the lime which is freed in the soil as the human bones disintegrate to form its shell. These snails live in warmer countries and they are called *Cecilioides* by scientists.

We ought to tell more about how mollusks move from place to place. Earlier, we said that some mollusks, especially the gastropods, move by using their "stomach foot" to crawl. Actually, land snails do not crawl on the ground itself. The large, fleshy foot has many glands which give off large amounts of slime or mucus. It is on this slime that the animals glide along, like somebody sliding on a thin layer of ice on a cold winter day. Or like an army tank which lays down its own track as it lumbers ahead, except that where the tank rolls up its track as it moves, the mollusk has to leave its trail behind. This appears on the ground in the form of a long, glistening, twisting, narrow, silvery ribbon. In olden times, some people believed that these trails were made by fairies in the night. But they are only the dried slime tracks of wandering snails.

We have also said that there are no flying mollusks. This is true. But a few mollusks are able to "fly" through water, so to speak. The cephalopods, the squids and octopuses, use a sort of jet propulsion and skim through the water apparently as easily, if not so swiftly, as a plane moves through the air. Sometimes, in fact, squid have been known to jet propel themselves so strongly under the water that they actually break through the surface and skid along almost like flying fish.

There is also a group of bivalves which appear to fly through the water, not like a jet plane but rather like a bird soaring through the air. These are the scallops or pectens which have a beautifully fluted, frequently brilliantly-colored shell. A species of *Pecten* shell is the trade-mark of a large gasoline company.

An octopus (cephalopod) (model).

When a *Pecten* is startled, it flaps its valves rapidly, almost like a bird ready to take off. It skitters along in the water, frequently changing direction, until it feels it is safe. Then it stops moving its valves and settles to the bottom. It is able to steer itself by keeping the mantle flaps closed except at a single spot. As the water is squirted out at this spot, the Pecten is steered in the opposite direction. When it wants to steer in another direction, it merely opens the mantle flaps at a different spot and squirts out the water. It is able to move with amazing swiftness.

Most bivalves live in mud or sand or burrow in wood or rock. Many, like the oysters, are solidly fixed to a hard surface. Since these mollusks move around very little or not at all, they do not need eyes, nor do they have any. But *Pecten* is an active bivalve,

A scallop shell (Pecten) showing the two rows of eyes.

A file clam (a bivalve) showing the fringed mantle.

which moves about a great deal. It needs to know where it is going. For this reason, the scallops are one of the very few groups of bivalves that do have eyes. They show up as a row of small, brilliant, blue spots, fixed to the edges of the mantle. It is not known just how much a *Pecten* can see, but the eyes are good enough to warn the mollusk when a bulky animal is approaching.

The file shell, also called *Lima*, is a close relative of the scallop. The valves of *Lima* have many small ribs, resembling those of a nail file. It has its mantle edge decorated with long, thin, waving tentacles. It is able to move much like *Pecten*.

The queen conch, a large sea snail living in Florida and the West Indies, has evolved a very strange way of walking. It, and its kin, use an organ which in most other snails has an entirely different purpose. Later, we will read about a little door or operculum which most marine snails use to protect the opening of their shell. This operculum fits snugly into the aperture or mouth of the shell and,

A queen conch showing the operculum which it uses for walking and defense.

when it is in place, serves beautifully to keep hungry predators away from the soft snail meat inside. In the queen conch, the operculum is quite small, far too small to close up the rather large shell aperture. When the queen conch moves along, it sticks out its foot to which the operculum is attached. It then fixes the pointed end of the operculum into the sandy or stony ground, like a ship's anchor. Then, by quickly pulling on its foot muscle, the conch leaps ahead like a small boy hopping on one leg. It can repeat this process rapidly and thus moves quite well, pulling itself along by its anchorlike operculum, so to speak. Incidentally, the sharp operculum can also give a painful pinch or even a cut to a finger that is carelessly placed inside the shell of a living conch.

HOW THEY REPRODUCE

Most mollusks hatch from eggs. A single oyster ejects millions and millions of eggs into the sea, only a few of which hatch out and survive. In the more advanced sea snails, the eggs are laid in various kinds of capsules which serve as a protection until the baby snails hatch. In most cases, the eggs are merely laid and the parents pay them no more attention—except sometimes to eat them! But in some advanced mollusks, like the cowries and the squids, the mother remains with the clutch until the young are born. While staying there, the mother seems to stir up the water frequently to remove debris and to provide the eggs with clean water.

Most land snails lay far fewer eggs than marine snails or fresh water snails. The eggs are buried in the ground, where they are less likely to be found by predators. Sometimes these eggs are enclosed in a hard shell. Most snails lay small to tiny eggs, but there is one kind of snail in South America and the West Indies which lays an egg as large as that of a pigeon.

In most cases, especially among the marine snails and bivalves, the eggs do not hatch directly into small snails or clams. Instead, minute organisms, which look quite different, appear. These are

26

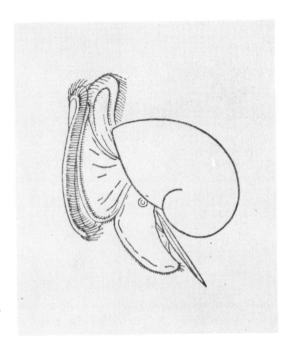

A gastropod veliger.

known as veligers, from the Latin words *vela* (veil) and *gero* (to carry), because they have swimming organs which look very much like tiny veils. The veligers swim about actively for a definite period of time, lasting from a few hours to a few days, weeks or even months. Finally, they have to settle on some hard object, such as a rock. If the veligers fail to find such an object, they fall into the mud and perish. For this reason, oystermen strew large quantities of broken shell on the bottom of their oyster beds. The veligers settle on these bits of shell and begin to grow into oysters. At this stage, they are known as spat. Of course, mollusks which normally live in mud or sand do not need to settle on a hard object. All they need is a favorable spot of sea bottom.

Sometimes the veligers settle on the shells of larger mollusks. Occasionally, abalone shells, for example, are found to be overgrown with the shells of other mollusks.

In some mollusks, the eggs do not hatch into veligers. They hatch directly into minute snails, resembling their parents. The

27

A land snail with eggs (pictured in insert) and young. Note slime-tracks.

baby snails are not taken care of or fed. They have to manage by themselves.

You may know that the shell of a crustacean like a crab or lobster does not keep expanding. In order for the animal to grow, it must shed its old shell, and a new, larger one is formed. This is soft at first, but eventually hardens. This process is called moulting.

Mollusks do not moult. They keep the same shell all their lives. As the mollusk grows, so does the shell, little by little. The new shell material is deposited at the edge of the shell by an organ called the mantle. The mantle can also deposit new patching material, if for some reason, the shell is broken. Snail or clam shells that have been repaired in this manner are frequently found.

Some people believe that a slug is a snail which has crawled out of its shell. This is not true. We have seen earlier that most cephalopods lost their external shells through evolution, so as not to be hindered by them. In the same way, for some reasons that are not quite clear, slugs are snails which, very long ago, gave up their shells and now live all their lives without one. Most slugs still have a tiny internal shelly plate, like the internal shells of cephalopods.

Most marine gastropods and all cephalopods are either male or female, like humans. These have to mate to fertilize the eggs. But in some marine gastropods and in most land snails, a single animal will be both male and female. These animals have to mate with one another, acting either as a male or as a female, before the eggs can be fertilized. In some fresh-water snails, one snail can act as the male for another snail, and it in turn can also be acting as a female for a third. This continues as snail after snail comes along, until finally, a long mating chain is formed of snails, each acting as both male and female at the same time.

Snails which are both male and female are said to be hermaphroditic. This word comes from combining the names of the Greek god Hermes, with the goddess Aphrodite. There is a very good reason for land snails being hermaphroditic. The land snails have the most difficult conditions of all mollusks in which to survive. Aquatic life is pretty easy: the water brings along the food and the oxygen needed for life, and removes the waste. The young are easily scattered over large areas. There generally are no rapid changes in temperature and the danger of the animal drying up does not exist. Because water is buoyant, it can support a strong, fairly heavy shell for the snail's protection. On land, the animal has to search for its food. Winter halts most life processes and the snail has to hibernate in order to survive. The young cannot easily move away from the place where they hatch and hence more and more animals must feed near the same spot. And the shells of land mollusks have to be light and thin enough to be carried easily. Therefore, they cannot offer very strong protection. There are still other reasons, but it is clear that life on land is a far more difficult business for a mollusk than life in the salty ocean or in fresh water.

With living conditions so difficult for the land snail, the chances for the survival of the colony are doubled when every individual snail can be a breeder of the young. Where the animals are separate in sex, only the female gives birth to young. The males do not. Among hermaphroditic animals, each one is a breeder. In this way, more young are born and the colony has a better chance of maintaining itself.

Strange as it may seen, not all mollusks are either male or female or even hermaphroditic. Some are actually male when they are young and become female as they get older. This is true of a snail that has a shell resembling a slipper. Slipper shells are commonly found in many places on our sea coasts. The young slipper shell starts out life as a male. After a while, he stops functioning as a male and, for a short time, is neuter. Finally, it turns female and remains so for the rest of her life. There are many other mollusks which go through the same process.

Before we leave the topic of how mollusks reproduce, we must tell about one more case in which the babies must live as parasites in fish before they can grow up properly.

Fishes caught in the fresh water of streams, rivers, ponds, and lakes may have many small black spots on their lips and gills and fins. At first, zoologists thought that these spots were parasites and called them parasiticum. Fishermen still call them blackheads, but they are not the result of disease. It is hard to believe, but the spots are actually the young of fresh-water clams or mussels, living inside the tissue of the fish.

Earlier, we saw that, when the eggs of clams hatch, little creatures called veligers appear. But this does not happen in the case of fresh-water mussels. The mother bivalve broods the eggs inside her gills until they are ready to be born. When they leave the gill brood-pouch, they already have two minute shells. These shells commonly have a small spine or hook at the edge. From the center of this tiny bivalve baby there extends a long, sensitive thread or filament. At this stage, however, the young creature does not resemble the parent clam. The shell looks very much like a small

30

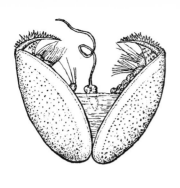

Left: *Glochidium of a fresh-water mussel.* Right: *A fresh-water mussel (bivalve).*

arrowhead attached to a thin, wavy shaft, the filament. For this reason, it was named glochidium (plural glochidia) from the Greek word *glochis*, arrowhead. Whatever its name, it is almost as different from a mature clam as caterpillar is from a butterfly. Its chief function is to become attached to the fins or gills of a fresh-water fish. If it does not become attached to a fish within a few hours after it leaves the mother, it perishes. But when it does come in contact with a fish, it quickly clamps its two shells together, and, with the hook, pierces the skin of the fish. In a short while, the skin of the fish grows over and covers the unripe mussel. It lives in this way as a parasite, being nourished by the tissues of its host. In about two weeks or a month, or frequently even longer, the little mussel is ready to take up life on its own. It frees itself from the fish—something like the way in which a butterfly escapes from a cocoon, and drops to the bottom of the stream. Here it begins to grow rapidly into a mature fresh-water mussel.

Some mussels have evolved a clever way to make sure that most of their glochidia babies will find a fish host and not drop to the mud and die. A part of the soft-bodied mantle of these mussels forms an appendage that resembles a small fish. As the clam takes in and expels water, this part of the mantle moves, making it seem that a small fish is struggling to free itself. When a real fish swims by, it is attracted by the movement of this fishlike lure. As it comes

31

closer, to see if this might be something that can be eaten, the mother mussel jerks in its mantle and shoots out a cloud of tiny glochidia. Before the fish can turn away, it already has hundreds of glochidia attached to its mouth, lips, and gills.

There seems to be a very good reason why a young mussel has to live like this after it is born. Adult bivalves cannot move very fast or very far. They are at the mercy of the river currents, which keep flowing downstream all the time. If the little clams were born anywhere along the river, they would all be swept downstream before they could anchor themselves in the mud at the bottom. The following year, when *these* clams gave birth, *their* young would be swept further downstream. After a short time, the whole clam population would be either living at the mouth of the river or else would be swept out to sea and perish. But the fresh-water mussels have evolved a method which insures that individuals could begin life upstream. Most fish can swim upstream against the currents. The glochidia living in the tissues of the fish then can drop off anywhere after they are fully developed. In this way, a good-sized clam population can be maintained in the upper parts of unpolluted rivers. Naturally, if for some reason all the fish in a stream or river die, the clams cannot reproduce and eventually disappear. Every mussel fisherman knows the motto: No fish, no mussels.

HOW THEY EAT

There are no creatures that have learned to eat in such an interesting way as the snails or gastropods. To understand this properly, we will have to use our imagination. Imagine then an animal which has changed its upper lip into a sharp, curved cutting blade. Its tongue is closely covered with rows and rows of tiny, sharp teeth. The sharp upper lip is called the jaw and the tooth-covered tongue is called the radula. This comes from the Latin word *rado*, which means to tear or mangle. In cephalopods the jaw is double and looks like a parrot's beak.

32

When the snail eats, it bites off a bit of food with the jaw. Then it passes the morsel on to the tongue, which moves forward and backward rhythmically, like a file. As it moves, the teeth tear the food particles into smaller and smaller bits. Finally, these are passed along by the radula, as on a conveyor belt, until they reach the gullet. Here they are swallowed. We, like most mammals, feed ourselves differently. We use our sharp front teeth to cut off a bit of food and the flattened ones in the back to crush and smash it to a mush, which we swallow.

Some gastropods do not have a jaw. They use their radula to scrape bits of algae directly from the rocks. If you watch a snail or chiton in a fish tank, you can see it using its radula in this way to scrape the green growths from the glass walls.

The snails' way of eating may not be much better than ours, but they do have one big advantage. New teeth are constantly being formed in rows at the back of the radula. As the rows of teeth in

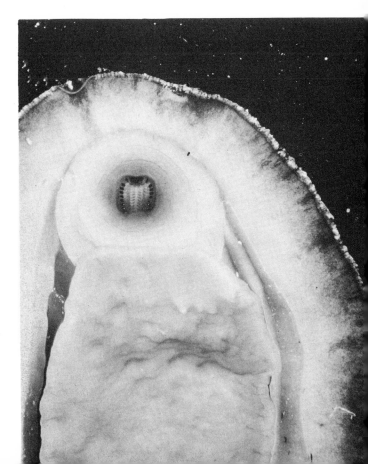

The open mouth of a chiton, showing the radula in use.

the front wear away and become useless, the hind ones move ahead and take their place. There is no need in the snail world for a snail dentist. He would starve to death! Would it not be handy if nature had provided humans with replaceable teeth? In another chapter we will talk more about the radula and some of the surprising uses to which it is put.

A radula is found only in mollusks. No other kind of animal is known to have such an organ. Five of the six classes of mollusks have radulas and all use them more or less in the same way. Some gastropods have become parasitic and live by sucking the blood and juices from host mollusks and other small animals. In this way, they are like the mosquitos and fleas who feed on humans and dogs. Because some mollusks have become adapted to parasitic feeding habits, they have lost their radula in the process of evolution. Instead, these species are provided with a sucking tube with which they pierce the outer skin of the animals on which they feed.

Bivalves are the only mollusks which do not have a radula. They eat in quite a different way. Most of them have two tubes called siphons. Through one of these a current of clean water with oxygen and tiny food animals is drawn in. Through the other one, a current of wastes is sent out. As the clean water comes in, it passes over the gills, where the fresh oxygen is exchanged for the used oxygen. But the gills also have another use. They are covered with a thin, sticky sheet of slime or mucus. On this slime sheet the bits of food are caught like flies on sticky fly paper. The mucus sheet with the trapped food is then passed into the stomach where it is wound up on a special organ, much like a sheet of cloth or a rope is wound up on a winch. The "winch"—called the crystalline style because it is as clear as crystal—helps to digest the food on the slime sheet. Sometimes one can find small, shiny rods floating around in an oyster stew that is being eaten. These are the crystalline styles from the oysters' stomach and they are very good to eat, since they are of great help to human as well as bivalve digestion. Some gastropods are also known to have crystalline styles.

For example, there is a gastropod which uses a slime sheet or thread of mucus to trap the food on which it lives. This is the worm shell or *Vermetus,* which lives in shallow waters in warmer seas. When *Vermetus* is born it looks like a proper young gastropod with a high spired, thin, quite pretty brown shell. For a time, it keeps growing quite regularly, but as it gets bigger, the shell changes completely in appearance. Instead of the new shell material being added evenly to the high spire, it grows away from the rest of the shell and begins to twist and wind like the tube burrow of a sea worm. This is why it is called a worm shell—which is also what *Vermetus* means. In time, *Vermetus* is nothing but a confused mass of shell tubing, running every which way. It also becomes fixed to some hard object like stone, coral, or another shell. In its hunt for food, the worm shell cannot move around like other gastropods. It is fixed for life—or until it is collected. Nor does it have the strange but convenient feeding tools of the bivalves. Instead, it flings out a large mucus sheet or long mucus threads from its opening, like a fisherman casting a net to catch fish. Tiny plants and other bits of food are caught on the sheet like a fish in a net. When enough food has been captured, the worm shell pulls in the loaded slime sheet with its radula. It is then passed into the stomach for digestion. Strange ways of feeding indeed!

One kind of clam has developed a rather interesting habit of feeding itself. This is the giant clam, found in the Pacific Ocean, of which we shall say more later. Like all clams, this one is able to eat only the tiny creatures and plants which it draws in with water. But the giant clam has evolved a way that insures there will always be food present when it has to eat.

It has a very large, colorful mantle which is commonly a brilliant bluish green. The fleshy mantle projects out of the shell when the clam is open, and vast numbers of tiny algae, on which the clam can feed, settle in the mantle. The clam has special organs which filter the sunlight in such a way that the algae grow and multiply very rapidly. When the clam needs food, it can harvest a meal from

35

the crop of algae which it has helped to grow. In this way, the giant clam is a kind of sea farmer.

THEIR ENEMIES AND HOW THEY DEFEND THEMSELVES

A snail or a clam seems to be a pretty helpless creature. Only the cephalopods are able to flee swiftly, or, if they are threatened, to fight back with tentacles and beak. They are able even to throw out a cloud of ink in which they can disappear. Sometimes the cloud of ink looks so much like a cephalopod that the attacker is fooled and goes for it while the real squid or octopus flees from danger.

But for most mollusks this is not so. When they are attacked, all they can do is close their valves tightly, if they are clams, or pull into their shells, if they are snails. Here their only hope is that the

Operculum or door in the aperture of a top shell (gastropod).

 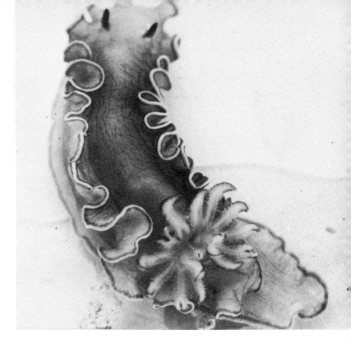

Left: *Venus comb* Murex *(gastropod)*. Right: *A nudibranch (a shell-less gastropod)*

attacker is too weak to get in and will finally become tired and go away. Most marine gastropods have a small door, called the operculum, with which they can tightly close the opening or aperture of the shell. Land shells generally do not have an operculum. Some land shells have instead a strong growth of toothlike projections in the aperture. This barrier seems to be big enough and strong enough to discourage most of the would-be snail-eaters, like beetles. But the best protection for a land snail is to hide. Most land snails come out only at night. In the daytime, they find refuge under rocks, bits of wood, or sprung bark of dead trees.

Some gastropods in the sea have developed very strong shell defenses. The rock shells (*Murex*) are so covered with long, sharp spines that most fish would not want to swallow them, no matter how hungry they are. Other shells are smooth but very strong and heavy. And still other snails, like the cone shells, as we shall see later, can actually sting and seriously injure or even kill an attacker.

Some of the most beautiful marine mollusks have no shells at all. They are sometimes called sea slugs but that is an ugly name for such beautiful creatures. Scientists call them nudibranchs, which means naked gills. The name is fitting because nudibranchs do not carry their gills inside their bodies as do most mollusks. Instead, their gills or branchia are generally placed along the surface of their backs. There they have many queer shapes like trees or corals or spikes or long tentacles. They are usually very brightly colored, as is the entire animal. It is a lovely sight to see a nudibranch slowly swimming along in the water, gracefully waving its foot.

If the nudibranchs do not have a shell, and are not able to escape their enemies by rapid flight, like a cephalopod, what protection do they have? Well, they have several. Some nudibranchs are the same color as the rocks, coral or seaweeds on which they rest. They blend in with their surroundings and are almost invisible. Others are brightly colored but have such a bad flavor that fish and other predators keep away. But still other nudibranchs have a much more interesting kind of defense.

In the sea can be found animals which look very much like flowers. They are called sea anemones. The arms of the anemone, which resemble the petals of a flower, bear a great many stinging cells. When a small fish bumps against one of these arms, the cells explode like a sea mine hit by a ship. As they burst, each cell shoots out a dart covered with poison. The poison paralyzes the fish and it is drawn into the anemone's stomach to be digested.

These stinging cells are very delicate. The slightest touch can set them off. Human beings who come into contact with them are painfully stung. Yet, in spite of this and in a way nobody understands, some nudibranchs are able to eat the anemones and yet keep the stinging cells unexploded. Furthermore, the cells are transferred from the stomach of the nudibranch to the tips of the naked gills. Here, these cells, which the sea anemone uses to obtain food, serve the nudibranch in a different way. Thus, if a predatory fish approaches such an armed nudibranch, the action of the exploding stinging cells drive the fish away. In this way, an ap-

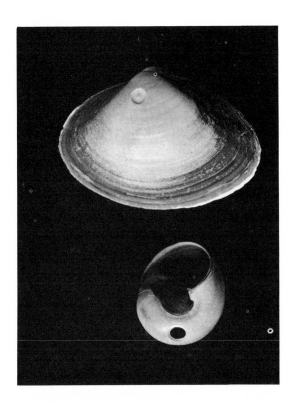

A bivalve and a gastropod, showing holes bored by the moon snail. One hole is not completed.

parently defenseless sea slug makes good use of a type of protection which was developed in an entirely different kind of animal.

Next to man, birds, small mammals, and some fish, the worst enemies of mollusks are other mollusks! Most primitive marine gastropods are herbivorous and live on algae and seaweed. But almost all the advanced sea snails eat meat. And the meat they seem to prefer above all others is mollusk meat.

These predators have many ways of breaking through the mollusk's defenses. Sometimes, as with the moon snails, they bore neat, countersunk holes through the shell and then devour the meat by pushing in a long snout or proboscis. The radula of these animals is near the tip of the proboscis. Sometimes little holes are drilled through oyster shells by the snail called the oyster drill. Oyster farmers lose a great deal of money from such attacks. Some rock shells have learned to break away the edges of a closed bivalve until enough room is made for the proboscis to be inserted. And then there are patient predators like the crown conch of Florida. When he comes across a sea snail for his dinner, and the snail is tightly locked behind its operculum, he merely sits down and waits. In time, the poor victim becomes tired or needs fresh oxygen or something. It opens its operculum just a tiny bit, and *wham!* The crown conch pushes the tip of its proboscis in. It quickly cuts the muscle which holds the snail in the shell so that the snail can no longer draw back. Then the meal begins.

Sea gulls like to eat large, meaty clams like the skimmer or surf clam. But the birds find that it is difficult to open the strong hard shells in which the meat is hidden. They cannot drill like some snails and their beak is not strong enough to open the valves or break the shell. They use a different way of getting inside.

When a gull finds a clam or digs one out of the sand where it is hiding, he seizes it in his beak and flies high over the hard sand or rocks on the seashore. Then he drops the clam and promptly swoops down to see what damage he has done to the shell. The shell hits the sand or rocks and splits open. Now, the gull can eat his dinner. Sometimes the gull is careless and drops the clam on a person's head by accident. The clamshell does not break open for the gull to have his meal—and the person can be hurt very badly or, at least, have a very sore head!

There is a wide concrete bridge between Far Rockaway and Atlantic Beach on Long Island, in New York State. This bridge has become a favorite place for gulls to break open the clams they want to eat, which has made the area dangerous for human beings. Automobiles are hit by falling clams and sometimes the roadway is covered by so many broken shells and slimy bits of clam meat that it becomes dangerous for motorists to travel on it. They should remember, however, that the gulls who cause all this annoyance are just naturally hungry and want to eat!

One of the worst non-molluscan enemies of bivalves is the inno-cent looking starfish. When it comes across a clam it would like to eat, it puts its five arms tightly around both valves. Then it applies its thousands of tiny sucking tube feet to the shell and begins to pull, slowly and steadily. It never lets up. At last, the clam becomes tired of resisting and the shell opens. The starfish now pushes its entire stomach into the clam meat and digests its meal on the half-shell, so to speak.

There is a story about starfish and oyster farmers which shows how dangerous actions based on ignorance can be. Long ago, when oyster farmers caught starfish in their oyster tongs, they were so angry at these pests that they chopped them into pieces and threw the pieces back into the water. Unfortunately for them, a starfish can grow back most of its lost parts. So, many times when a starfish was cut up, several of the pieces began to regenerate the parts they had lost. In a short time, the oyster farmer who thought he had killed one dangerous starfish, had really turned a single enemy into two to five very much alive ones who were dining on his oyster crop.

4

Superstitions About Mollusks

THE SOUND OF THE SEA IN SHELLS

Is it true, that if you put a large sea shell against your ear, you can hear the roar of breaking surf? This is a very pretty idea. Many people believe it and many poets and writers have been inspired by it. Unfortunately, it is not correct. Doctors can tell you why you *seem* to hear the sea's roar in a sea shell, but it is not necessary to ask them. All you have to do is perform a simple little experiment.

Take any good-sized empty gastropod shell, such as a large *Murex* or a giant African snail and hold the opening against your ear. You will hear a soft roaring sound, like waves breaking in the distance. Now take a teacup or drinking glass or even hold your cupped hand lightly against your ear. You will hear the same sound. Any hollow object will do as well as a sounding board. You don't need a shell.

OYSTER PEARLS AND PEARL OYSTERS

Everybody knows that pearls of great price come from oysters. And there are people who eat a great many oysters on the half shell, hoping to find a valuable pearl and become rich for the rest of their lives. They are bound to be disappointed, even if they do find a pearl. As a matter of fact, they will be lucky if they do not break a tooth "finding" it!

The facts are that valuable pearls come only from a special kind of large pearl oyster, called *Pinctada,* found in tropical seas. The shells of these oysters are beautifully iridescent inside, like the colors seen on a large soap bubble. The pearls sometimes found inside the mantle have the same lovely sheen. But oysters we eat in restaurants are entirely different. Their shells, called *Ostrea,* are dull and chalky and pearls formed in them are not shiny and beautiful. They are of interest only to students of oysters. It should be understood that all of the various kinds of bivalves can produce pearls, but only those of the tropical pearl oysters are of commercial value.

THE "MAN EATER"

We have seen that the radula is an important organ which enables mollusks to "chew" their food before swallowing it. Only the bivalves, of all six classes of mollusks, do not have radulas. They get their food by siphoning it up when they "breathe" in the water. Their food consists of microscopic animals and plants of many kinds. Clams cannot digest big chunks of food. Nevertheless, people still publish warnings about the dangerous "man-eating"

A giant clam (Tridacna) *on a coral reef at low tide.*

giant clam in the South Seas. There is no man-eating clam.

There is indeed a huge clam living in the coral reefs in the far Pacific, which we have already mentioned. The valves are generally white and have three or more wavelike projections which fit tightly together. Thus the name, *Tridacna*, meaning three-biter, was applied to it. It is one of the largest members of the entire mollusk group. Only the giant squids, which live in very deep water, are larger. Some *Tridacna* have been found which were more than four feet long and weighed more than 500 pounds. They are frequently used in churches as baptismal fonts. And yet these huge creatures can eat only the same tiny things that the smallest clams eat, nothing larger.

Why is it then that some people insist on calling it a man-eater? The reason is not hard to find. When the large *Tridacna* is undisturbed, it opens both valves and keeps siphoning water in and out, to breathe and eat. In this situation, it is possible for a careless diver to get his hand or foot wedged between the two huge valves. This startles the clam, which immediately pulls the two valves strongly together for protection from the intruder. If the diver cannot free himself, he will drown. But the clam is just as "unhappy" about all this as the poor diver. It cannot eat him or enjoy him in any way at all. It wishes to get rid of him as soon as possible, but instinct forces it to keep its valves closed. When the clam finally gets tired and begins to relax the muscles which keep the valves tightly closed, the diver is already dead, drowned in the rising tide.

This is the source of the "man-eating" story. Divers may have lost their lives in this way, but certainly very rarely. People who know *Tridacna* well, say it is difficult to get one's limbs caught like this. The valves of *Tridacna* do not react as rapidly as the jaws of a bear trap. There should be plenty of time for a diver to get away, even if he does step on an opened *Tridacna*. But we cannot say that such an accident has never happened. At any rate, it is incorrect to talk about "man-eating" clams.

5

Some Curious Mollusks

HOMING MOLLUSKS

There are certain mollusks which have developed some very curious habits in their way of living. The limpets, as we have said, are gastropods with shells which are not twisted, but instead, look like Chinese hats or small inverted cups. The limpets all have a large, flat foot with which they cling strongly to a rocky surface. When disturbed, they cling so tightly that it is hard to remove them from the rock without breaking the shell.

Limpets eat at night, when the tide is in and they are covered with water. They move around on the rock that is their home and, with their very strong radulas, scrape off the algae and seaweeds growing there. But when the tide goes out, they return to the very spot that they were on before. Here they nest until the next high tide comes along. In some cases, the same limpet has occupied the same spot for such a long time that it has actually hollowed out a

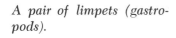

A pair of limpets (gastropods).

shallow depression in the rock which exactly fits its shell. We all know that pigeons have a very strong homing instinct. So do some mollusks.

THE SEA SNAIL IN CORAL

Another mollusk has an even more curious habit. This is a sea snail called *Magilus*. It is a relative of the *Murex* or rock snails and lives on coral reefs in the Pacific and Indian Oceans. Not only does it live on them, it actually lives in them. How does it do this without being "choked" to death as the coral grows?

When it is very small, it settles on a reef of live coral. As the coral grows and becomes thicker, the little *Magilus* stays fixed to the same place. But to avoid being covered and choked by hard coral, it just keeps the walls of its opening or aperture growing out until it forms a long and rather strong shelly tube. In time, the twisted main shell of *Magilus* is hidden far inside the coral reef but the long tube keeps the snail in constant touch with the water from which it draws its food and oxygen. Here it lives snugly and well protected. When the *Magilus* shells are collected, they look like white, short, stubby walking sticks. The twisted shell at one end is like the handle and the tube forms the stick part. *Magilus* is a mollusk which lets the coral animals build a protection for its house.

Magilus *in its burrow in a reef-coral.*

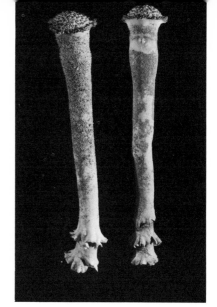

Two views of a watering pot shell (Brechites). *Note tiny bivalve.*

THE WATERING POT CLAM

In the shallow mud of many lagoons in the South Seas there can be found a very curious shell that does not look like a mollusk shell at all. But it really is. It is called the watering pot shell and it looks like the sprinkler on an old-fashioned watering pot. Malacologists call it *Brechites*. It consists of a long hollow tube, open at one end and capped at the other with a cover which has many tiny holes like a sprinkler. Sometimes there are pretty white fringes along the open end.

Although one would never guess to look at it, this is a true bivalve. After it is born, the veliger turns into a tiny bivalve, with two little shells which, for a while, grow normally. But, suddenly, the edges of the shells begin to grow toward one another until they touch and join into a single piece. From this point on they grow into a long tubelike object. The two original small shells of the young watering pot can be seen at the base of the tube. In another kind of watering pot shell, only a single shell can be seen. Although this mollusk is quite interesting and well worth keeping in a shell collection, it is not very pretty. It is dull and dirty white in color. It looks like a hollow, thin-walled animal bone.

47

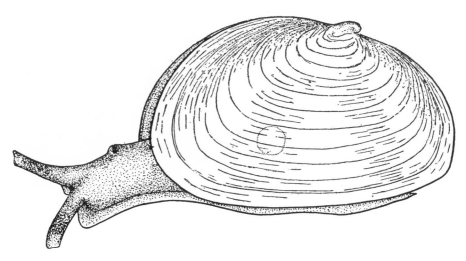

The bivalve-gastropod Berthelinia.

THE BIVALVE-GASTROPOD

In 1959, a Japanese scientist, Dr. Kawaguti was examining a tiny green bivalve living on some seaweed. Suddenly, the two valves opened, but instead of a clam's foot coming out, which is what usually happens in the case of a bivalve, the scientist was amazed to see the head and tentacles of a little gastropod appear. A gastropod in a bivalve shell? It was almost like seeing a dog's head, ears, teeth and all coming out from the shell of a turtle! Dr. Kawaguti could not believe his eyes. He was afraid to publish a report about this curious creature because he was sure that no one would believe him. People would say that he was imagining things, dreaming— or worse. But when the scientist saw more and more of these bivalve-gastropods, he called in his friend Dr. Baba, and together they published a report about this curious mollusk. Soon other malacologists in other parts of the world began finding similar animals, which are now known as *Berthelinia*. These gastropods occur on seaweeds in warmer waters from Africa, India, Australia, and Japan all the way to California and Panama and the West Indies.

These fantastic mollusks are not very large and not particularly pretty. They are usually less than one-half inch long and the shells are thin and very fragile. At the outer part of the hinge there is a small, twisted spire, a left-over of the single gastropod shell the animal had when it was born and before it began to form the two bivalvelike shells.

THE GASTROPOD-BIVALVE

Now, if there is a true gastropod which looks like a bivalve, wouldn't it be only fair to have a bivalve which looks like a gastropod? And strange as it may seem, there is one indeed. This is a small animal living on the coast of California. It is a true bivalve and does have two shells. But the shells, instead of being on the outside to protect the animal's soft parts, are hidden away inside the creature, like the shells of a slug or a cephalopod. It moves around vigorously by using its foot, much as the foot of a gastropod is employed. Although it is very minute animal, it has been given a rather long and hard name. It is called *Chlamydoconcha*, meaning cloaked shell. So we have two strange mollusks, a gastropod-bivalve and a bivalve-gastropod.

THE COLLECTOR SHELL

While we are speaking about strange shells like *Brechites*, the watering pot, *Magilus*, *Berthelinia*, the bivalve-gastropod and *Chlamydoconcha*, the gastropod-bivalve, we should also mention the very curious collector shell. This gastropod lives in Florida and other areas of the world where the ocean water is always warm. It is called the collector shell because it goes about collecting the shells of other mollusks which happen to live in the same area. Of course, it does not collect them because they are beautiful or interesting. It has an entirely different purpose. When it is growing and the shell matter is forming at the edge of its shell, the mollusk,

Top and bottom views of a collector shell (Xenophora).

with the edge of its mantle, takes a dead shell which it has found nearby and holds it against the part of the shell being formed. In a short while, the dead shell is firmly fixed in place and stays there as a part of the collector shell. This snail also uses broken bits of shells or even pieces of rock or coral in the same way. The result is that, after the collector has grown to a nice large size, anybody looking at it from above would never guess that he is looking at a snail shell. It looks like an untidy little pile of shell rubble. No snail eater would guess that there is a possible meal for him hiding underneath. The scientific name for the collector snails is very meaningful. It is called *Xenophora* from the Greek words *xeno*, a stranger, and *phora*, a carrier. (Remember Mono-placo-phora, the single plate carrier?) And this is what it really is. It is really not a collector at all. It is a bearer of strange bits of another creature on its shell.

50

6

Useful Mollusks

MOLLUSKS WHICH WE EAT

Man has always found many uses for mollusks. We eat clams and oysters and some snails, like the abalone of California. The Europeans eat many more mollusks, including land snails. Mussels and squid and octopus (cephalopods) are eaten with much pleasure in the lands around the Mediterranean Sea. In other parts of the world, even more mollusks are eaten. They form an important part of the human diet.

THE WINDOW-PANE OYSTER

In the Philippine Islands and elsewhere in Southeast Asia, an oyster shell is sometimes used in place of window glass. This shell, called *Placuna,* is very thin and looks like cloudy glass. One cannot see through such a "glass," but light passes through it fairly well. It is a relative of the jingle shells found on many American beaches. These also have a very thin shell through which light can pass. The *Placuna* shell is used to decorate jewelry and cigarette and jewel cases in this country. They are also cut into circular disks and hung together on individual strings. When the breeze blows, the disks strike each other and make a very pleasant tinkling sound. Recently, so many *Placuna* shells were being used for these purposes that the governments of some nations became afraid that all of these window-pane oysters would be wiped out. Now there are laws to protect them.

51

DYE FROM MOLLUSKS

In ancient times, certain *Murex* or rock shells in the Mediterranean Sea were crushed and the juices from their bodies were used to dye cloth. The color which came out was a very beautiful, rich, reddish purple. It was called Tyrian purple because much of it was made in the city of Tyre, in Asia Minor. Tyrian purple was used by the emperors of Rome for their own garments, so it was called royal purple. Roman senators were permitted to wear togas with a purple edge. Common people were not allowed to wear clothes dyed this color at all. Because only the emperors and nobility could make use of the purple, the expression "Born to the Purple" came to mean a child born of a noble family.

THE ROYAL COWRIE

In the Fiji Islands, a very lovely gastropod shell called the golden cowrie is found. It is around three or four inches long—about the size of a pear—and the surface has a large orange or golden area. This shell is rare even today. In ancient times, before the white man came to the Fijis, only the chiefs of the tribes were permitted to wear this cowrie on a necklace as a sign of royalty. Commoners were not permitted to wear it. Hence we can imagine that perhaps the Fiji Islanders had an expression like "Born to the Cowrie," which to them might have meant the same as "Born to the Purple" did to the ancient Romans.

SHELLS USED AS MONEY

Not only were cowrie shells important as a sign of royalty. Some of them were used as money in the South Seas until rather recent times. There were two kinds of cowries commonly employed in this way. One is called the money cowrie, even today. The other is called the ringed cowrie because it has a thin orange line forming an oval ring on the top. People were able to buy food, such as

52

pigs and vegetables, and weapons and kitchen utensils with their cowrie money. In some islands, they could even buy their wives.

In what is now New England, before the white man came to America, the Indians used wampum for money. This they made of beads which were cut out of the purple and white parts of the hard shell clam. Belts made of wampum were also used to send coded messages. This was done by arranging the colored and white beads in the form of symbols. On the West Coast of the United States, elephant-tusk shells (scaphopods) were strung on strings of plant fiber and also used as money.

MOLLUSK SHELL ORNAMENTS

Shells are so beautiful that they always have been worn as ornaments, even by primitive man. They are made into necklaces, bracelets, earrings, and nose rings in the South Seas. Shells are also used there to decorate buildings and canoes. Slivers cut from shells are set into furniture decorations. Many people in America and elsewhere still use mollusk shells to decorate themselves. Shell necklaces are frequently brought home from the West Indies by returning tourists, and shell jewelry is a popular item in department stores in the United States. The beauty of shells has never gone unnoticed.

The most expensive mollusk ornament of all is the pearl. The most valuable pearls come from pearl oysters. The pearl is formed when a bit of irritating sand grain, shell fragment or tiny parasite becomes lodged in the mantle of the oyster. Just as our eyes tear when they are irritated by a cinder, in a similar way the mantle of the oyster also begins to "tear." But the oyster's tears do not flow down and away. They harden around the irritating object and, in time, may form a valuable pearl.

In nature, only very few oysters are found with pearls inside, but the Japanese have learned how to put a bit of irritant into the mantle of an oyster purposely and thus force every oyster so treated to produce a pearl. The pearls that are produced in this way are called cultured pearls. They are just as beautiful as "natural" ones, because they are made in exactly the same way, by the "tears" of the oyster. Colorful pearls also are found in some marine snails, such as the pink ones formed by the queen conch.

MOLLUSKS IN RELIGION

At least two mollusks have become revered objects in religion. Pious Christians in the Middle Ages used to make pilgrimages to the Holy Land. When they returned, they were permitted to wear a scallop shell found in the Mediterranean Sea to show that they had been pilgrims. Even today, this scallop is named after St. James of Spain, where he is called San Diego or Santiago.

Vishnu is the name of one of the gods of the Hindus. He is shown holding a special kind of shell in his hand. This is called the chank shell and it is considered to be a holy object by the Hindus. Sometimes a freak chank shell appears. The usual chank shell has its aperture or opening on the right side. If one is found with the opening on the left side, it is considered to be especially sacred. Some Hindu doctors believe that medicine given from such a left-handed chank shell works much better than medicine given any other way.

SILK FROM MOLLUSKS

Most of the uses of mollusks which we have written about up to now are not too unusual. But it is surprising to find that there is a kind of bivalve which produces a thread that can be woven into gloves and scarves. The bivalve is a large, triangular clam which lives in Florida and other warm areas of the world. It is called *Pinna* and looks like a large Japanese fan which is not completely closed. *Pinna* lives more than half-buried in the mud on the bottom of bays and inlets. To keep its position, it fastens the buried point of the "fan" to a sunken rock or other hard object. It does this by

A Pinna clam (2), and its byssus (1), and a glove made of Cloth of Gold (3).

spinning a kind of thread called a byssus.

People have learned to collect this byssus and weave very beautiful pieces of cloth with it. Cloth made this way has a dark, shining appearance and looks like gold. For this reason, the material is called Cloth of Gold. Certain other bivalves such as the ordinary blue sea mussel also spins a byssus but the thread is too short to be used for weaving. Most people know that silk comes from a caterpillar called the silkworm. They are surprised to hear that a clam can also spin a kind of "silk" thread.

7

Unpleasant Mollusks

SNAILS IN DRINKING WATER

Up to now, we have been speaking about beautiful, interesting, or useful mollusks. Now we will describe a few mollusks which are either a mild nuisance or actually dangerous to man.

Toward the end of the last century, residents of the United States who lived in Chicago, Cleveland, Buffalo and other cities on the shores of Lake Michigan and Lake Erie, had a very disturbing experience when they turned on their faucets to get drinking water. Nice clear water did indeed flow out, as they expected, but together with the water, they also found living snails in their glasses! Although these snails were not offensive in any other way, their presence alone and their large numbers made them a nuisance. Some naturalists in these cities must have been delighted to be able to collect interesting snails so easily, right in their own kitchens. But most people were horrified or disgusted. It is hard to get used to seeing snails swimming in the water you are drinking.

The results of an investigation proved to be very interesting. Somehow or other, a small, rather pretty, fresh-water snail from Europe was introduced into the waters of Lake Erie in the late eighteen seventies. Conditions were good and the snail population grew very rapidly. Soon these mollusks were found nearly everywhere in Lake Erie and Lake Michigan and the streams and rivers connected with them. They finally got into the water mains of the cities and towns which used Lake Erie water for drinking. And so live snails appeared unwanted in kitchen sinks and washbasins.

56

Giant African Snail

The people were not annoyed by sharing their baths with snails for very long. Screens were put in front of the water intakes and the snails were stopped before they got into kitchens and bathrooms. But the snails accumulated in such numbers around the screens that they had to be cleared away regularly. It is no longer a pest in the waterworks.

The scientific name for this snail is *Bithynia,* but most Americans still call it the faucet snail, in memory of its first appearance in the United States.

THE GIANT AFRICAN SNAIL

Most snails eat things which humans do not want, so people do not get angry at such mollusks. But sometimes mollusks eat the same food that humans like. These mollusks we call pests and they become our enemies. We try to keep their numbers down or even kill them all off. We have already written about oyster drills and other creatures that dine on the oysters and clams which we would like to see on our own tables. Now we will meet a few pest mollusks which eat the plants and flowers we grow for ourselves.

The people living in Southern California and Florida are greatly

57

bothered by some species of land snails which eat and destroy many plants and flowers in their gardens. Much money and effort is spent in fighting these snails, not always very successfully. But the worst snail of this kind is the giant African snail, called *Achatina.*

Why is this snail a much greater pest than the other plant-eating mollusks? Most pest snails are small, the smallest ones being under one quarter of an inch in length and the larger ones no longer than about an inch. But the giant African snail is a huge fellow. He can reach a length of six inches, with his girth that of a very large pear or turnip. Because of its size the African snail eats a great deal more food than its smaller relatives do. Moreover, it has untidy habits and is a menace to health. It spreads its slimy trail wherever it goes. It likes to live in garbage heaps and when it moves away it spreads bad smells and germs everywhere. When it dies and decays, it produces a very disagreeable odor and attracts flies and other troublesome insects.

Originally, as the name tells us, this snail lived in Africa. Little by little, it spread to the islands of the Indian and Pacific Oceans. When it showed up in Ceylon, it completely destroyed the tea crop. During World War II, the Japanese brought it to the western Pacific islands, to serve as food. When the Japanese left, nobody wanted to eat the snails and their numbers increased greatly. Now *Achatina* is a serious pest in Guam, Saipan, Hawaii and elsewhere.

The Department of Agriculture at Washington, D. C., forbids the importation of *Achatina* and most other live snails into mainland United States. Agents of the department carefully examine all plants that are imported, to make sure that no small *Achatina* or their eggs are accidentally brought along. In spite of this, *Achatina* suddenly appeared recently in large numbers in North Miami, Florida. Agents worked hard to exterminate the animals before they would spread to other areas and cause much damage to crops. This shows more than anything else how important it is for everyone to be on guard constantly against the introduction of molluscan pests from other parts of the world.

Of the unpleasant snails we have mentioned so far, one was a nuisance in kitchen sinks and the other a pest which eats plants. Although this makes them unpleasant, they are not really dangerous. But now we want to point out a snail which is a serious health menace to millions of people living in the warmer areas of the world. It is the most dangerous snail of all. Like the mosquitos which spread malaria and other serious diseases, this snail carries a very serious illness to huge numbers of people. Millions of residents of Africa, Asia, the West Indies and other areas suffer from it and thousands die every year. They do not die of the illness itself, but they are so weakened by it and their resistance is so much lowered that they perish when they fall victim to other diseases.

Doctors have two long names for this disease. It is called either Bilharzia or Schistosomiasis. But most people simply call it snail fever. You may wonder how the snail transmits this disease to human beings. We know that malaria is transmitted when an infected mosquito bites a person. But snail fever works differently. The snails live in ponds and slow-flowing rivers, as well as in the flooded fields where people in the tropics grow rice. In the same water there also lives a parasite or fluke. This fluke goes through a complicated life cycle. At one stage of its life it has to enter the body of a special kind of fresh-water snail. Inside the body of the snail, like the baby fresh-water mussels we have already read about, the fluke changes its form. When it is ready, it leaves the body of the snail and now it must enter the body of a human being. It does this by piercing the skin of anybody who happens to be in the water where it lives. It is so tiny no one feels anything as the parasite forces its way in. Once inside, it gets into the bloodstream and other parts of the human body. As a result, the person attacked becomes very sick.

While living in the human body, the fluke lays millions of eggs.

Now, in many tropical countries, human wastes are not well disposed of and the eggs of the parasite find their way freely into the streams and lakes. Once the eggs reach the water, the entire cycle begins again.

In order to eliminate the disease either the snails have to be wiped out or sanitary conditions must be improved. Only in this way can the life cycle of the fluke be broken and the disease prevented. In the costly battle against snail fever, scientists and engineers are using both methods.

We know that governments throughout the world spend much money to fight malaria and yellow fever. It is not so well known that almost as much money is used to fight snail fever.

We have been speaking of a single kind of fresh-water snail as the host of the fluke. Actually, there are at least three kinds. In the West Indies, snail fever is transmitted by a wheel snail, in Africa by a relative of the wheel snail with a higher spire, and in Asia by a rather small, slender snail, a member of an entirely different family of snails.

Fortunately, so far, snail fever has not been found in mainland United States. Although the wheel snail which transmits the disease has been seen in Louisiana and parts of western Florida, there are no people living there who suffer from the disease. Therefore, these snails are not infected by the flukes that cause snail fever.

However, there is a different kind of snail fever which is found in the vicinity of some lakes in Michigan and Wisconsin. People who go bathing in these lakes suffer from a skin infection called bather's or swimmer's itch. The itch is caused by a relative of the snail fever fluke. This relative does not live and lay its eggs in a human being. Instead, it uses some kinds of water birds, like ducks, for the same purpose. When this fluke comes in contact with a bather, it tries to pierce the skin, and enter the human's body anyway, but it does not succeed in doing this and soon perishes. In its efforts to get through the skin, however, it causes an annoying and itching rash.

60

There are a few last words to be said about this very unpleasant parasite of snails, birds, and mammals. One type of fluke attacks sheep. When it gets into the body of a sheep, it destroys the liver tissues and the sheep dies of a serious disease called liver rot. This disease has caused extensive losses to sheep farmers in England and elsewhere.

CLAMS WHICH DESTROY WOODEN PIERS AND SHIPS

The Sacramento River in California is one of the most important rivers on the West Coast of the United States. It empties into San Francisco Bay, which connects with the Pacific Ocean. In 1920, the State of California suffered from a long drought. Very little rain fell during the entire year. In addition, much water was drawn from the river to be used to irrigate the many new farms in the area. The result was that the river shrank in size and more and more salt water from the Pacific Ocean began to enter San Francisco Bay. Salt water appeared where there had been only fresh or slightly brackish water before.

Suddenly, all the wooden wharves, piers, and warehouses which had been built many years before along the coast of the bay began to collapse. Hundreds of thousands of dollars worth of property was destroyed. Why did this happen and what did the lack of rain have to do with the destruction?

It may be hard to believe, but the villain was a small ocean

The tube of a shipworm (Teredo) in a piece of wood.

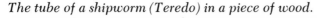

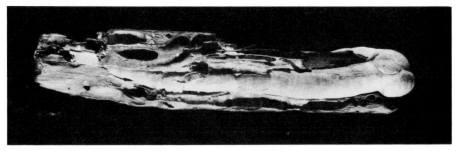

61

bivalve called *Teredo*. This clam is mistakenly called a shipworm, for it is not a worm at all. It is a true little clam with the conventional two valves but with queer habits, some of which are very costly to ship and pier owners.

As soon as the *Teredo* is born, it settles on a piece of submerged wood and begins to bore. It does this by holding on with its disc-like foot and slowly rocking its two shells against the wood. The shell surface is covered with many fine, sharp ridges, like a file. The clam apparently feeds on the fine fragments of wood after they are rasped off the interior of the bore hole. As the hole or burrow gets deeper and deeper, the *Teredo* lines it with a thin, smooth layer of limy shell material. In time, it has built a long, deep, curving burrow in which it lives for the rest of its life. Hundreds and even thousands of teredos can attack a single piece of timber and soon it becomes hollowed out inside, like a house-beam attacked by termites. This generally happens suddenly and without warning. The reason is that, although *Teredo* burrows are rather large and easily seen when the wood in which they appear is broken open, the point at which each *Teredo* enters is very tiny. The outer surface shows no sign of the destruction going on within. Shipworms are sometimes called termites of the sea.

Teredo has another organ which keeps it safe inside its snug, shell-lined burrow. Ot the very tip of its long, wormlike body, where *Teredo* is in constant contact with the sea-water, there are two tiny objects shaped like paddles. These paddles are called pallets. If for any reason the water around the entrance to the burrow becomes dangerous to the *Teredo* inside, the entrance is simply closed off by the pallets. Thus the pallets in a way are like the doors or operculums of sea snails, of which we have read previously. They make it hard to kill *Teredo* with poison.

Through the ages, thousands of wooden ships and piers have been destroyed by these clams. The only way to protect the wood is to keep the young *Teredo* from settling in it. This is done in various ways. The wood is either coated with poisonous paint or covered entirely with copper sheeting. Sometimes hot tar is forced into the pilings under tremendous pressure so that it penetrates the entire piece of timber. The tar is unpleasant to the larvae of *Teredo* and they stay away from it. Of course, *Teredo* cannot bore into ships made of steel or iron.

From what has been written here, it can be seen that *Teredo* is not a very popular creature. It seems to cause nothing but damage to human beings by attacking their piers and ships. In fact, it seems to do no good at all. But this is not altogether true. Teredos also do something useful. Sometimes huge pieces of timber or even large trees are swept into the ocean by storms and occasionally wooden barges sink in shallow water. These submerged wooden objects are especially dangerous to smaller boats which can collide with them at night or in a fog and are either damaged or sunk. *Teredo*, by its habit of attacking all kinds of wood, whether useful or dangerous, soon weakens these threats to navigation and eventually destroys them. For this reason they can be called scavengers or sanitation forces of the ocean.

One more thing about *Teredo* is interesting to know. Most of them live and destroy wood only in very salt water. Any harbor which has a large river flowing into it has water which is not salty enough for *Teredo* to survive in it, unless, as happened in California, the salinity of the river is increased because of drought.

There are close relatives of *Teredo* which can indeed live in fresh water and which also can cause damage to wooden structures there. One lives in Australia, and another is found in a lake in Panama.

THE SNAIL WITH THE DEADLY BITE

Several years ago, a young man was collecting shells on a little island near the Great Barrier Reef of Australia. He picked up a large living cone shell and, with a knife, began to scrape away the outer skin on the shell surface, to see the pretty colors underneath.

63

Shell and animal of the poison cone snail (model).

Suddenly, he felt a sharp sting on the palm of his hand. He saw a small puncture there and the area near the puncture felt numb. In about ten minutes, there was a stiff feeling around his lips and, a little later, he was unable to see very clearly. Soon he could not move his arms and legs. One hour after having been stung, the young man became unconscious and a few hours later he was dead.

There are many more cases of people being stung while they handled cone shells. The natives of the shores where such shells can be found are very much afraid of them and avoid them as much as they can. Many people who were bitten were treated quickly by a doctor and recovered, but many others died.

How does the cone shell inflict such a bite? Earlier in this book, we wrote about the radula of snails, the tooth-covered "tongue" with which the animal tears its food to bits for swallowing. The cone shells also have a radula but is quite different in appearance from that found in most snails. Instead of having one made up of many small teeth like a file, the cone shell radula is composed of a few long, slender, needlelike teeth, each one armed with a harpoon-shaped hook at the tip. The teeth have a hollow channel and when the harpoonlike point pierces the skin of a victim, a small quantity of a very toxic poison is injected. To many people, this poison is only a little less dangerous than that of a rattlesnake.

The poison teeth of the cone shells are used mostly for gathering food. When a fish or a worm or some other food animal is near, the snail quickly shoots out the pointed teeth, like an Eskimo harpooning a seal. The poison paralyzes the victim and the cone shell pulls the animal into its mouth, which opens very widely. In a moment, the food is completely swallowed.

The main purpose of the peculiar radula is to provide food. But, as we have seen, it can also serve as a means of protection and attack against bigger enemies of the cone shells.

There are about three hundred different kinds of cone shells in the world, all of them living in tropical and subtropical seas. But no more than half a dozen of them are known to be poisonous to man. Most of these dangerous snails live near the shores of the Indian and Pacific Oceans, in the Far East. It so happens that all of these venomous snails have shells which are very beautiful and much prized by collectors. Of course, once the animal has been killed and removed from the shell, the shells are perfectly safe to handle. It is only those which still have the living animal inside that can cause harm.

Cone shells are not the only mollusks with a poisonous bite. Recently, it was discovered that a small octopus living along the shore of California is also capable of inflicting a poisonous bite. Other octopuses, big and small, also seem to be able to do this. Therefore, it is wise to be very careful when one handles live octopuses—that is, if one really wants to handle them at all!

8

Shell Collecting

HOW TO COLLECT SHELLS

Mollusk shells, especially those which are formed by marine snails, are frequently very colorful and attractively formed. Many naturalists, as well as artists, consider them to be the most beautiful objects in nature. People have collected shells from the earliest times because of their beauty. Today, there are many shell collectors who are ready to pay high prices for particularly rare and handsome shells. Some private collections are worth a great deal of money.

The most popular shells among collectors—and those for which the best prices are paid—are the volute shells, the cone shells, the cowrie shells, and the rock shells. The most exquisite kinds come from the tropics and subtropics, especially the Indian and Pacific Oceans and the Caribbean Sea. The golden cowrie, which comes from the Fiji Islands, sells today for about $300, but the glory-of-the-sea cone shell can bring $2000 or more for a large, well-preserved specimen. Several other kinds of attractive cowrie shells are known, represented so far, by only a handful of specimens. Until more are found, these rare shells will be regarded as priceless. Many of the most valuable shells are to be seen today only in the collections of large public museums.

Numerous collectors buy their shells from dealers, who obtain them from fishermen. Securing shells for collectors has become an important sideline for the fishermen of the Philippines, Australia, and especially Japan. A few wealthy collectors become impatient with this method of getting shells. They charter yachts and set out

Examining a bed of sea mussels.

on shelling expeditions of their own. Many new and wonderful kinds of mollusks have been discovered for the first time by such collectors.

But even in less favorable waters than the tropics, a number of interesting and even beautiful mollusks can be collected. Some tiny shells are lovely objects when they are seen through a microscope. Forming a collection of all the mollusks of a certain region, whether on the beaches, in the rivers and lakes or on land, is a very interesting hobby. Sometimes these collections prove of value to science, and a person who started out as a shell collector in his neighborhood might very well become a professional malacologist later.

Such collections, whether amateur or professional, can be in-

67

creased by exchanging shells with collectors in other areas. In this way, not only is the collection made richer and more interesting, but delightful personal contacts can be made.

There are several ways to look for shells. The easiest of all shells to find are the ones that occur on beaches. They usually are scattered by the tides and winds along the high water mark and can be picked easily. Such collecting is especially good after a strong on-shore storm. If you want to collect the tiny shells as well, it is best to take home drift material from this high water line and then examine it under a magnifying glass.

Of course, most of the shells collected this way will be dead, beach-worn specimens. If you want to collect live mollusks, you must know where to look for them. We have already said a little about where mollusks live, but now we must go into more detail.

Some mollusks burrow in beach sand and these can best be collected at very low tide. A little experience soon tells under what bump in the sand one will find a live moon snail, surf clam, or, in Florida and California, an olive shell. Low tide is also a good time to collect mollusks which live on rocks and jetties. In the daytime, most of them are found in seaweed and on the underside of the rocks and, in tropical waters, under blocks of coral. To get the mollusks which live in deeper water, one has to use dredges or go skin or SCUBA diving. The mollusks found this way are less commonly gathered, therefore these deeper water species are rarer in collections. On mud flats of inlets and bays, the mollusks which live there in huge numbers can be picked off the mud or sand surface. In fresh water such as ponds, lakes, and rivers, where there are no regular tides, living mollusks can generally be found in shallow water by dredging in the mud bottom. This is not as complicated as it might sound. An ordinary soup strainer of any size is good enough to obtain the mollusks living in the mud. A stick firmly tied to the strainer makes it possible to dredge in deeper water. One should also examine the undersides of floating leaves, wood, and other bits of debris.

Elana and Kenny looking for land shells.

Of all the different kinds of shell collecting, finding land shells is the hardest work. In the daytime, these snails live under leaves, rotting wood, rocks and any other kind of hiding place. Some even live in trees. It takes much grubbing and sifting, or lots of tree climbing, to find them. It is easier to collect land snails at night or after a rain storm. This is the time when they come out to feed and mate. At night, one can find them with the aid of a flashlight or a kerosene lantern.

Not only can land shell collecting be hard work, it can also be dangerous. You have to be on constant watch for poisonous insects and snakes. Even where there are no such real dangers, you can come into contact with poison ivy and poison oak and suffer painful skin rashes.

Marine shell collecting in tropical and subtropical waters also can be dangerous. There are fire corals, and jelly fish, and sea anemones or nudibranchs which sting, long-spined sea urchins which prick, moray eels which nip off toes, and sharks and hungry fishes which have sharp teeth or fins. But in places like New England and other more northern areas, marine shell collecting is nothing but fun—unless one steps into a deep hole and can't swim!

When live mollusks have been collected, the soft animal parts must be taken out of the shell. All of the soft body must be removed or else the parts left behind will decay and become quite unpleasant to the sense of smell of anyone in the vicinity. They remain so for a very long time and make the collector very unpopular with any other people who live in his house.

Large snails and all bivalves can be cleaned by quick boiling in water first. Then the animal's soft parts are carefully removed with a bent pin or some other kind of hook. This is not always easy to do and takes much care and practice. If a part of the animal remains stubbornly in the shell and cannot be shaken out, it sometimes helps to soak it for a few days in alcohol. Then it is left to dry FOR A VERY LONG TIME! If the snails are too small to let the animal be removed, they can be soaked, shell and all, in alcohol and left to dry.

HOW TO ARRANGE A SHELL COLLECTION

Now that you have the specimens, what do you do with them? How do you arrange them so that they can be shown and studied? First you must provide each series or lot of shells with a neat label. A series or lot represents one or more specimens of the same kind or species of shell which were collected at the same time at the same locality or place. Where several different species are collected at one place, there should be several different lots of shells. The label should have room for the popular and scientific names of the species, the place where it was collected, the time and date when it was collected, and a few words about the conditions under which it was living, such as "in mud," "in seaweed on a rock," or whatever.

70

The fun and fascination of shell collecting may be found in the small but carefully selected, arranged, and labeled "finds" of the amateur, as well as in the huge collections to be seen by enthusiasts in many museums. Here, Author Emerson is shown holding a spiny oyster, one of the more than two million scientifically arranged shells included in the collection of the Department of Living Invertebrates at The American Museum of Natural History, of which he is Curator and Chairman.

Finally, the label should have the name of the collector.

In addition, every complete label will also have a catalog number. Careful collectors keep a catalog book in which all the different lots of shells are given a number in the order in which they are added to the collection. A ledger book or a loose-leaf binder may be used for this purpose. The catalog book also has written or typed on it all the information which has been copied on the label. The catalog number is written, not only on the label but also, in India ink, on the shell or shells of each lot. If a shell is small or tiny, it should be put in a small shell vial, together with the number, printed or typed on a piece of paper. The main reason for having a catalog and numbers is to make sure that, if the collection is upset, you will be able to match the shells with their proper labels. It also tells you how many *lots* of shells—not *species* are contained in your collection.

There are several ways to identify the specimens that you have just collected. The easiest is to get an illustrated book of shells and look for a picture of the shell you have gathered, with its name and description. Some may be pictured in this book. Many other books can be found in public libraries or they can be bought, some very reasonably.

Of course, you must be sure to look in the proper books. For example, it is useless to look for a land shell in a book dealing only with marine shells. Or for a shell which is found only in Florida in a book about the shells of Australia. Many shell books deal with the shells from definite areas, like the east or west coasts of America, Japan, the Caribbean Sea, and so on. Others deal with shells from larger areas, such as the Indian and Pacific Oceans, the Atlantic Ocean. Europe, or the Mediterranean Sea. Certain books present only the shells found in a limited region like southern Florida, the New York City area, Massachusetts or California. Other books do not limit themselves to such areas, but rather take up all the shells of certain families, wherever they live, like cone shells, cowries, rock shells or volutes. However, there are many books which cover all kinds of shells—land, fresh water and marine —from all over the world. Such are perhaps the best for beginners.

There are also other ways of learning the names of shells. You can take unnamed shells to a museum and compare them with the specimens on display there. Sometimes, if he is not too busy, the curator of mollusks in the museum will be willing to help. Or you may join a local shell club, if there is one, and ask the other members to help identify the shells.

When looking in books for shell names, it is important to remember that most books give only the scientific or Latin name of the shells. These names look very hard for those who speak English to pronounce and remember. They are frequently long and strange and, at first, it seems they can never be learned. But that isn't true. People of foreign parentage may have long and difficult names, but, if our friends have such names, we learn them quickly enough. Most Latin names are no more difficult than Spanish or Polish names, for example, and some are even easier and quite pretty. For instance, the queen conch of Florida is called *Strombus gigas* because it is so large, and the crown conch is called *Melongena corona* because it resembles a crown. But by whatever name you call your shells, whether by the common English name or the Latin scientific name, they remain just as beautiful and interesting, and give just as much pleasure.

The best method of housing a shell collection must be determined by each individual collector. Any kind of suitable cabinet or set of drawers will do. Some books explain how special shell cabinets and shell drawers can be built. Each series of shells—that is, each lot having the same catalog number—and its label, should be kept in an individual container. Small cardboard trays are commonly used, and these can be made at home with a little cardboard and glue. Shells may also be kept in small plastic boxes of various sizes. Such boxes may be bought in many hardware stores. They are better than cardboard trays because they keep the specimens free of dust—and they are washable.

Sometimes collectors keep live mollusks in fish tanks or vivariums and spend much time observing them. In this way they learn a great deal about how mollusks live, feed, mate, lay eggs and so on. In many cases not even scientists know everything about these subjects. The observant collector might possibly contribute useful knowledge to the field of molluscan science.

But above all we have said so far about collecting live mollusks, there is one important point that should never be forgotten. It is well to remember that these creatures also have the right to live. If its life is taken from one of them, this should be only for a good purpose. When a shell has a carefully written label it becomes forever a valuable scientific specimen which any museum would be glad to own. But when the shell lies around without a label, its life was taken from it for no good purpose at all. It is a useless specimen as far as science is concerned. Such a mollusk has not been collected, it has been killed wastefully. It is never wise to collect more live specimens than one can use immediately. In America, the laws of some states prohibit the collecting of living mollusks or limit the numbers of certain species that may be taken after a license is obtained.

Of course, none of this applies to shells collected dead on a beach. You may take as many as you want. You are hurting no one—except maybe another collector who wants the same shells! And you can always swap with him. But make him copy your labels carefully.

Once a collection is well established and steadily growing, the fortunate shell collector has a marvelous hobby which can stay with him all his life, enriching it and filling it with endless thrills. Through knowledge gained by studying this field of natural science, he will find a greater enjoyment and understanding of the complicated natural world around him.

The truly fortunate collector is the one who, beginning to collect shells in his youth, decides to make their study his life's work. We think the happiest people in the world are the ones whose hobby is also their profession.

Glossary

abalone—a'-ba-loan-ee, a type of gastropod mollusk with a large foot
Achatina—a-ca-ti'-na, the giant African snail
anemones—a-ne'-mo-nees, flower-like sea animals
annelids—an'-ne-lids, segmented worms
Berthelinia—ber-the-lin'-ia, the bivalve gastropod
bilharzia—bil-har'-zia, snail fever
Bithynia—bi-thin'-ia, the faucet snail
Brechites—bre-kite'-tees, the watering-pot mollusk
byssus—bis'-sus, the thread spun as holdfasts by some bivalves
Cecilioides—ce-cil-i-oi'-des, the graveyard snail
cephalopods—sef'-al-o-pods, the octopuses and squids, etc.
chitons—kite'-tons, the shell made up of eight overlapping valves
Chlamydoconcha—clam-me-do-kon'-ka, the gastropod bivalve
conch—konk, a large sea-snail
crustaceans—crus-tay'-shuns, class including lobsters, crabs, etc.
gastropods—gas'-tro-pods, snails and slugs
glochidium—glow-kid'-dium, larvae of fresh-water mussels
hermaphroditic—her-maph'-ro-di-tic, an animal which is male and female at the same time.
hibernate—hi'-ber-nate, to pass the winter in a kind of sleep
Janthina—jan'thin-na, the violet snails
Magilus—ma-jill'-us, a kind of rock snail (Murex)
malacologist—ma-la-co'-lo-jist, a zoologist specializing in the study of mollusks
Melongena corona—me-lon-jean'-na co-ro'-na, the crown conch
Monoplacophora—mo-no-pla-co'-phor-a, the segmented mollusks
Murex—myu'-rex, the rock snails
nudibranchs—nyu'-di-brancks, the sea slugs
Ostrea—o-stray'-a, the edible oysters

75

Pecten—pec'-ten, the scallop shells
Pinctada—pink-ta'-da, the pearl oyster
Placuna—pla-coo'-na, the window-pane oyster
predator—pre'-da-tor, an animal that preys on other animals for its food
proboscis—pro-bo'-sis, the snout of a snail
radula—ra'-dyu-la, the tooth ribbon of most mollusks
scaphopods—ska'-fo-pods, the elephant-tusk or tooth shells
schistosomiasis—shi-sto-so-my-a-sis, snail fever
Strombus gigas—strom'-bus, ji'-gas, the queen conch
Teredo—te-ree'-do, the shipworm
Tridacna—try-dac'-na, the giant clam
veligers—ve'-li-jers, the larvae of mollusks
Vermetus—ver-mee'-tus, the worm snail
Xenophora—zee-no'-pho-ra, the carrier or collector snail

Index

Morris K. Jacobson

received his MA degree in Germanistics at Columbia University, in New York. Since 1930, he has taught foreign languages in high schools of that city and, for the last seventeen years, has been chairman of the Department of Foreign Languages of Andrew Jackson High School, in Queens. A frustrated biologist, he became interested in mollusks when he moved to Rockaway Beach, New York. He has collected everywhere in this general area and has also made several collecting trips to Cuba, Mexico, Jamaica, Puerto Rico, Central America, and several of the Lesser Antilles. He recently donated a considerable collection of shells to The American Museum of Natural History, where he is an Associate in Malacology.

Mr. Jacobson was one of the founders of the New York Shell Club, served as its first president, and edited its *Notes*. He was also president of the American Malacological Union and is the editor of its *Annual Reports*. Besides writing the handbook, *Shells of the New York City Area* with Dr. William K. Emerson, he is the author of about fifty specialized articles on mollusks.

William K. Emerson

is curator of Mollusks and Chairman of the Department of Living Invertebrates at The American Museum of Natural History, in New York City. He is in charge of the invertebrate collections, including more than two million scientifically arranged specimens of mollusks. A native of California, Dr. Emerson received his Ph.D. from the University of California at Berkeley. He is the author of nearly one hundred scientific papers in the field of malacology and is a specialist of the marine gastropods and the scaphopods (tusk shells). He has collected extensively along the Pacific and Atlantic coasts of the United States and has made numerous field trips by land and sea to the west coast of Mexico and to the Caribbean region.

Dr. Emerson has served as the president of the American Malacological Union and of the Western Society of Malacologists. His biography is listed in "American Men of Science" and "Who's Who In America."